Nature's Changes

Metamorphosis

Changing Bodies

Bobbie Kalman

Crabtree Publishing Company

www.crabtreebooks.com

Nature's Changes

Created by Bobbie Kalman

Dedicated by Bryan Kivell
With love to Mom, Dad, Adam, and Lesley

Editor-in-Chief
Bobbie Kalman

Writing team
Bobbie Kalman
Kelley MacAulay
Kathryn Smithyman

Editors
Molly Aloian
Robin Johnson
Reagan Miller

Design
Margaret Amy Reiach
Samantha Crabtree (cover)
Robert MacGregor (series logo)

Production coordinator
Katherine Kantor

Photo research
Crystal Foxton

Consultant
Patricia Loesche, Ph.D., Animal Behavior Program,
Department of Psychology, University of Washington

Illustrations
Barbara Bedell: pages 16, 17, 28, 29, 31
Antoinette "Cookie" Bortolon: page 15 (top)
Katherine Kantor: page 24
Margaret Amy Reiach: series logo illustrations, pages 9, 11,
     12, 14, 15 (bottom-left and right)
Bonna Rouse: pages 4, 18-19, 20, 21, 22, 23

Photographs
© Dwight Kuhn: pages 11, 13 (left), 25
Robert McCaw: page 23
Minden Pictures: Rene Krekels/Foto Natura: page 24
Photo Researchers Inc.: G. I. Bernard: page 22; Andy Harmer: page 27;
     Jim Zipp: pages 12, 13 (middle and right), 14
Visuals Unlimited: Bill Beatty: page 20; Patrice Ceisel: page 21;
     Gary Meszaros: page 26; Dick Poe: pages 8, 10 (top)
Other images by Brand X Pictures, Corel, Digital Stock,
     Digital Vision, and Otto Rogge Photography

Crabtree Publishing Company

www.crabtreebooks.com   1-800-387-7650

Cataloging-in-Publication Data
Kalman, Bobbie.
    Metamorphosis : changing bodies / Bobbie Kalman.
    p. cm. -- (Nature's changes series)
Includes index.
    ISBN-13: 978-0-7787-2273-1 (RLB)
    ISBN-10: 0-7787-2273-2 (RLB)
    ISBN-13: 978-0-7787-2307-3 (pbk.)
    ISBN-10: 0-7787-2307-0 (pbk.)
    1. Metamorphosis--Juvenile literature. I. Title.
QL981.K35 2005
571.8'76--dc22
                                          2005000491
                                             LC

**Published in
the United States**

PMB16A
350 Fifth Ave.
Suite 3308
New York, NY
10118

**Published
in Canada**

616 Welland Ave.,
St. Catharines, Ontario
Canada
L2M 5V6

**Published in the
United Kingdom**

73 Lime Walk
Headington
Oxford
OX3 7AD
United Kingdom

**Published
in Australia**

386 Mt. Alexander Rd.,
Ascot Vale (Melbourne)
VIC 3032

Contents

Big changes

Most animals begin their lives inside eggs. Many animals look like their parents when they **hatch**, or break out of their eggs. These animals do not change very much as they grow.

baby sea turtle

Sea turtles are animals that do not change very much as they grow.

adult sea turtle

What is metamorphosis?

Some animals look nothing like their parents when they hatch. As these animals grow into adults, their bodies go through many changes. These changes are called **metamorphosis**. Metamorphosis means changing **form**, or shape.

This caterpillar will go through metamorphosis. When it has finished metamorphosis, it will look like the beautiful butterfly on the right.

5

Two kinds of changes

There are two kinds of metamorphosis.
One kind is called **complete metamorphosis**.
Insects that go through complete metamorphosis
change completely. They have four stages
in their lives. The four stages are egg, **larva**,
pupa, and adult. Insects such as butterflies and
ladybugs go through complete metamorphosis.

butterfly

ladybug

Three stages

The other kind of metamorphosis is called **incomplete metamorphosis**. Animals that go through incomplete metamorphosis have only three stages in their lives. The three stages are egg, **nymph**, and adult. Dragonflies and grasshoppers are insects that go through incomplete metamorphosis.

This dragonfly is an adult.

Butterfly eggs

Butterflies go through complete
metamorphosis. A butterfly begins
its life as a tiny baby inside an egg.
The baby looks like a little worm.
In its egg, the baby has food to eat.
The food is called **yolk**.

A tiny baby insect is growing inside this butterfly egg.

Eggs on plants

Different kinds of butterflies lay their eggs on different kinds of plants. For example, monarch butterfly mothers lay their eggs only on milkweed plants. If there are no milkweed plants, there will be no monarch butterflies!

A monarch butterfly has laid one egg on each of these milkweed leaves.

A larva grows quickly

After three to six days, the baby hatches from its egg. It chews its way out. It is now a larva. A butterfly larva is called a **caterpillar**. After hatching, the caterpillar eats its egg. The egg is full of **nutrients**. Nutrients help living things grow.

This monarch caterpillar is eating its egg.

Caterpillar bodies

There are many kinds of caterpillars. Not all caterpillars look the same. Some caterpillars are green, some are red, some are yellow, and some have stripes. Different kinds of caterpillars change into different kinds of butterflies.

Room to grow

A caterpillar is hungry! It has strong jaws for chewing leaves. It eats a lot and grows quickly, but its skin does not grow with its body. Eventually, its skin becomes too tight. The caterpillar must **molt**, or shed its skin. As it keeps eating, its body gets even bigger. The caterpillar grows and molts several times.

This monarch caterpillar has just finished molting. Its old skin is behind its body. The caterpillar eats its old skin because the skin contains many nutrients. Not all caterpillars eat their old skin.

Becoming a pupa

After many molts, a caterpillar gets ready for the next stage in its metamorphosis. It makes a strong string called **silk** inside its body. The caterpillar uses the silk string to attach itself to the branch of a tree. It then hangs upside down from the branch and molts one last time.

Inside the chrysalis

After the last molt, a hard case forms around the caterpillar's body. The case is called a **chrysalis**. Inside the chrysalis, the caterpillar's body changes completely. It turns into liquid. The insect is now a pupa. Little by little, the pupa grows body parts such as wings. It is changing into an adult butterfly.

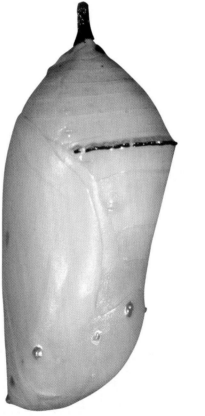

A chrysalis starts to form around the caterpillar's body.

Inside the chrysalis, the caterpillar's body is liquid.

When the chrysalis turns clear, the caterpillar has finished its metamorphosis. The adult butterfly is ready to break out of the chrysalis.

An adult butterfly

When the butterfly is fully formed, it pushes itself out of the chrysalis. It cannot fly yet because its wings are wet and weak. The butterfly hangs upside down from the chrysalis until its wings are dry and strong. The adult butterfly then flies away.

A new body

The caterpillar has now finished metamorphosis. It has changed into a butterfly. Look at the pictures below to see how the caterpillar's body has changed.

proboscis

The caterpillar

- walked on stubby legs
- did not have wings
- had strong jaws for chewing leaves
- had a long, thin yellow body with black and white stripes

The butterfly

- has six thin legs
- has two pairs of wings
- has a **proboscis** for sucking a sweet liquid called **nectar** from flowers
- has orange wings with black lines and white spots

Ladybug changes

A ladybug is a kind of beetle. It is another insect that goes through complete metamorphosis. Keep reading to learn how a ladybug's body changes as it goes through complete metamorphosis.

Inside the egg

Mother ladybugs lay groups of eggs. The baby ladybugs inside the eggs are in their first stage of metamorphosis. Each baby eats the yolk inside its egg and grows.

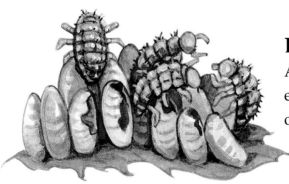

Life as a larva

A tiny larva hatches from each egg. Each larva goes off on its own to find food. A ladybug larva eats **aphids**. Aphids are tiny insects. As the larva grows, it molts four times.

Pupa in a chrysalis

After its last molt, the larva attaches itself to a plant's leaf or stem. It makes a chrysalis around its body. Inside the chrysalis, the larva's body turns into liquid. The insect is now a pupa. Its adult body parts start to grow. When the pupa has all its adult parts, it breaks open its chrysalis.

Fly away, ladybug!

The adult ladybug pushes itself out of the chrysalis. It now has wings and can fly. The ladybug eats aphids, just as it did when it was a larva.

Frog changes

Frogs go through complete
metamorphosis. The changes
in the bodies of frogs are very
different from the changes in
the bodies of insects.

eggs

tadpoles

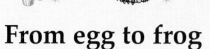

From egg to frog

Frogs begin their lives inside eggs. When they hatch, they are not frogs, however. They are **tadpoles**. As tadpoles go through metamorphosis, they become frogs. Some frogs go through metamorphosis in a few weeks. Others can take several months to finish metamorphosis.

frog

This tadpole will soon be a frog.

tadpoles

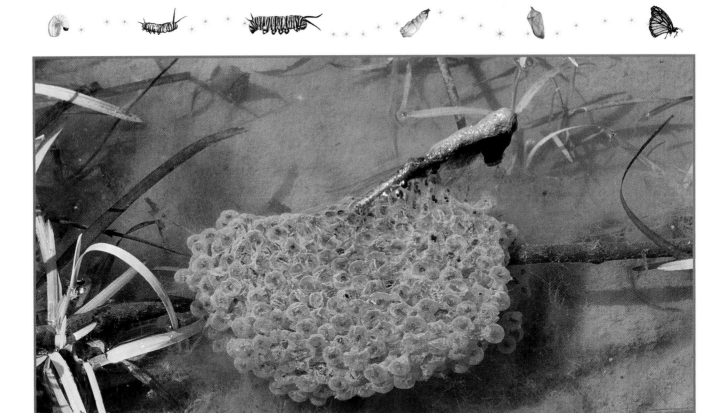

Eggs called spawn

Frogs lay their eggs in calm, shallow water. The eggs stick together in clumps. Clumps of frog eggs are called **spawn**. There can be thousands of eggs in a clump of spawn. The eggs look like balls of clear jelly. The jelly helps protect the tiny babies growing in the eggs. Some of the babies will become tadpoles.

Most of the eggs laid by a mother frog will never hatch. They will be eaten by turtles, fish, and other animals.

Time to hatch!

After about a week, a tadpole hatches from each egg. A tadpole has a head and a tail. It breathes through body parts called **gills**, just as fish do. At first, the tadpole cannot swim well. It rests on weeds or on other plants. As the tadpole grows stronger, it begins to swim around looking for tiny plants to eat.

A tadpole swims by moving its tail from side to side.

More tadpole changes

After the tadpole starts swimming, its body begins to change. The tadpole grows legs on both sides of its tail. As its back legs grow, its tail starts to shrink. Skin begins to cover its gills, and **lungs** form inside its body. Lungs are body parts that take in air and let out air. Soon, the tadpole grows front legs.

A tadpole uses its tiny teeth to eat insects and plants.

Becoming a frog

tadpole with a small tail

When its tail is almost gone, the tadpole looks more like a frog. It lives at the edge of a pond. It sometimes uses its new legs to crawl out of the water to look for insects to eat. The tadpole uses its lungs to breathe air. When its tail is completely gone, the tadpole has become an adult frog.

adult frog

A frog has strong legs for jumping and a long, sticky tongue for catching insects.

Dragonfly metamorphosis

Dragonflies are insects that go through incomplete metamorphosis. Dragonfly mothers lay their eggs in water or on plants near water. Some kinds of dragonfly babies grow inside their eggs for a few weeks. Other kinds of dragonfly babies grow inside their eggs for a few months.

A dragonfly mother lays her eggs in water. She lays many eggs at a time.

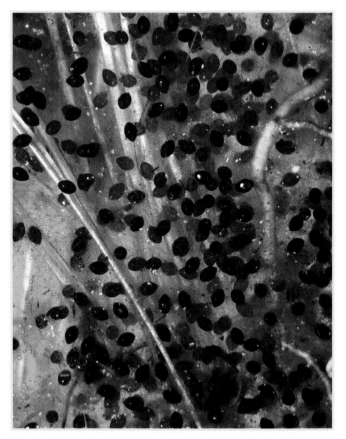

Some of these dragonfly eggs will be eaten by other animals, but many will survive.

Living under water

A nymph hatches from each egg. It lives under water. It paddles its six legs to swim. The nymph breathes using gills. It has a mouthpart called a **mask**. The nymph stretches out its mask to grab food. It eats tiny insects, fish, and tadpoles. The nymph in this picture is eating a tadpole.

Eating and growing

A nymph eats a lot of food and grows quickly. As the nymph grows, lungs form inside its body. The nymph now needs to breathe air above water. It moves near the top of the water, where it can stick its head up to get breaths of air.

Many molts

As the nymph grows, its skin becomes too tight. The insect molts many times. After its first molt, the nymph begins to grow tiny wings. Each time the nymph molts, its wings grow a little bigger.

Tiny wings are starting to form on this dragonfly nymph's back.

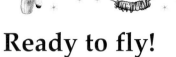

Ready to fly!

Just before the nymph becomes an adult, it crawls out of the water and climbs onto a plant. On the plant, the nymph molts for the last time. It is now an adult dragonfly. Its wings are soft and wet. They are folded up. The dragonfly sits on the plant and unfolds its wings. When its wings become hard and dry, the dragonfly is ready to fly.

This nymph is molting for the last time. It is crawling out of its old skin. Its wings are wet.

The adult dragonfly is leaving its old skin behind. Its wings are unfolded and dry.

Grasshopper changes

A grasshopper is another insect that goes through incomplete metamorphosis. When a baby grasshopper hatches from its egg, it is a nymph. As the nymph grows, it changes into an adult grasshopper.

Eggs in soil

A mother grasshopper lays her eggs in soil. She covers the eggs with a white liquid that she makes inside her body. The liquid gets hard when it dries. It keeps the eggs warm. A baby grasshopper grows inside each egg.

These grasshopper eggs are safe and warm in the soil.

A growing nymph

A tiny nymph hatches from each egg. A nymph looks like an adult grasshopper, but it is smaller and does not have wings. Soon after a nymph hatches, its wings begin to grow. Each time the nymph molts, its wings grow larger.

This grasshopper nymph has small wings. The nymph is not yet able to fly.

An adult grasshopper

An adult grasshopper has big, strong wings. It can fly around to look for food. Adult grasshoppers eat a lot of plants.

This adult grasshopper's wings are strong enough for flying.

Watch it change!

You have learned that metamorphosis means "a change of form." You can see animals change right before your eyes by making moving pictures. Read the instructions on the next page to learn how to make your own moving metamorphosis picture!

Choose an animal

Before you begin, look at the pictures in this book again. Choose an animal for your moving picture. You will need to draw two pictures of the same animal. One picture should show the animal before it has finished metamorphosis. The other should show an adult animal that has completed its metamorphosis.

Making moving pictures

1. First, cut two small squares out of a piece of paper.

2. Use pencil crayons to draw the two pictures. Draw one picture on one square and the other picture on the other square.

3. Once you have finished your drawings, tape your pictures back to back on the end of a straw or a pencil.

4. Hold the straw or pencil between your hands. To see your animal change shape, quickly rub your hands together to make the pictures spin.

Words to know

Note: Boldfaced words that are defined in the text may not appear in the glossary.

chrysalis A hard covering that forms around the body of an insect during the third stage of complete metamorphosis

gill A body part that takes oxygen from water

larva An insect that is in the second stage of complete metamorphosis

molt To shed a layer of skin

nutrient A substance that helps living things grow and stay healthy

nymph An insect that is in the second stage of incomplete metamorphosis

pupa An insect that is inside a chrysalis during the third stage of complete metamorphosis

spawn A mass of fish or frog eggs

Index

1 2 3 4 5 6 7 8 9 0 Printed in the U.S.A. 4 3 2 1 0 9 8 7 6 5